Boardsailing

a beginner's manu

second edition
Charles Wand-Tetley ● John Heath
photographs by Tim Hore

Fernhurst Books

Contents

© Fernhurst Books 1986

First published 1981 by
Fernhurst Books, 53 High Street, Steyning, West Sussex
Second edition published 1986

ISBN 0 906754 22 4

Composition by A & G Phototypesetters, Knaphill
Printed by Ebenezer Baylis & Son Ltd, Worcester

Foreword

Windsurfing is the sport of today. It is challenging and exhilarating for newcomers and experts alike. Its ease and enjoyment have made it a compelling sport for people of all ages and physiques.

Learning the basics properly doesn't take long and can lead to hours of safe enjoyment. This book details the most up-to-date method of learning to windsurf which has been developed over years of teaching the sport in the UK and abroad. Combined with a practical course at an RYA recognised school, with a qualified instructor and the right equipment, you will be sailing within hours.

Much helpful information is contained within these pages, aiming to make the sport safer for you and everyone around you. Remember: a little common sense regarding your own safety can help to prevent accidents that might lead to unwanted legislation against the sport.

Enjoy this book, and discover the magic of the sport of windsurfing.

Phil Jones
National Boardsailing Coach

Acknowledgements

The publishers would like to thank Goren Nyman of Windsurfing UK, importers of the Sailboard, for his kind assistance in the preparation of this book, and Phil Jones, National Boardsailing Coach, for his valuable advice on the manuscript.

Thanks are also due to Mark Woods who posed for many of the photographs, which were shot at the Dinton Pasture Country Club, Winnersh, Reading and from the Sigma 33 'Insignia' in the Solent.

The cover photograph is by Phil Holden and the cover design is by Behram Kapadia.

1 Choosing a board

One of the great things about boardsailing is the simplicity of the equipment; you can rig your board in a few minutes and you don't have to be Superman to cope with it on your own.

The board shown here is a typical modern sailboard; other makes are very similar and can be rigged more or less as described here – see the manufacturer's instructions for variations.

A sailboard consists of an unsinkable board powered by a rig consisting of a mast, sail and boom. The rig is joined to the board by a pivoting mast foot which allows the rig to be angled in any direction.

The board itself has a nonslip surface, and several features on the deck; a large hole for the daggerboard and a small one for the safety leash plus a hole or track for the mast foot. It may also have footstraps for strong-wind sailing.

The skeg on the underside helps the board sail in a straight line. The daggerboard stops the board being blown sideways; it may be a pivoting type, retracting (i.e. disappears up into the hull) or simply have an up-and-down action.

The mast foot is inserted into the track or socket in the board. It should be adjustable because getting the correct fit between the mast foot and board is as vital as the adjustment of a ski binding – it must be loose enough to release if your leg is trapped between the mast and the board, but tight enough so that the mast doesn't keep jumping out. Note that many boards have mast tracks fitted so the rig position can be adjusted while sailing. If the mast foot does release, the safety leash prevents the rig floating away.

The sail has a sleeve sewn on the front edge, through which you slide the mast. Some sails are stiffened by battens pushed into pockets in the back edge of the sail.

The rig is held together by three ropes – the inhaul attaches the boom to the mast, the outhaul pulls the back corner of the sail to the end of the boom; the downhaul fastens the mast to the mast foot as well as pulling down the front edge of the sail.

The uphaul is a rope used to pull the rig out of the water. Fix the free end to the mast foot with a length of elastic to keep it always within reach.

The wishbone shape of the boom allows you to control the rig from either side.

Choosing a board

Before choosing a board, think about your plans for using it. Are you buying it for all-round family use on holiday, or do you plan to sail it

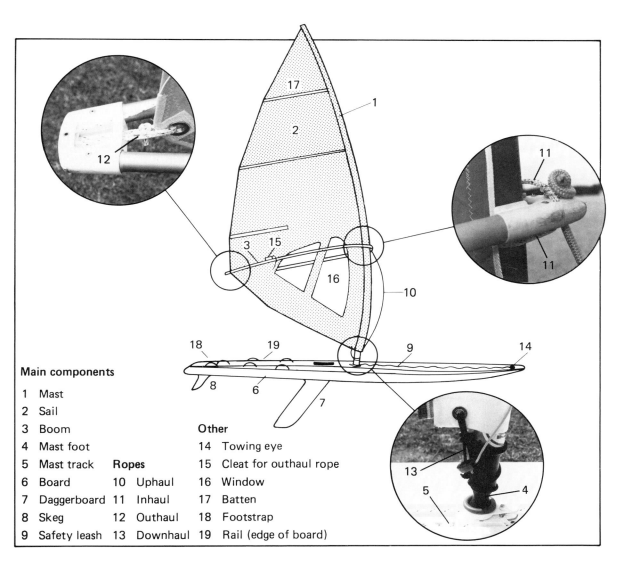

Main components

1 Mast
2 Sail
3 Boom
4 Mast foot
5 Mast track
6 Board
7 Daggerboard
8 Skeg
9 Safety leash

Ropes
10 Uphaul
11 Inhaul
12 Outhaul
13 Downhaul

Other
14 Towing eye
15 Cleat for outhaul rope
16 Window
17 Batten
18 Footstrap
19 Rail (edge of board)

yourself every weekend? Will you be on the sea or inland? And finally, how much can you afford?

The board

Volume
This is a measure of the support the board will give you. The heavier you are, the more volume you need. A lightweight beginner requires 180 to 200 litres of volume, while those of more ample proportions should think of 220 to 240 litres. Most beginner's boards are 3.5 to 3.75 metres long.

Tail shape

Boards with square tails are more stable than those with round tails, though they have less scope for high-speed manoeuvres. Don't choose too ambitious a shape to start with.

Construction

There are several ways of building a board.

- Polyethylene (with a foam core) is cheapest, toughest and a good material for a first-time board.
- ABS and ASA (with foam core) is slightly more fragile, but lighter in weight.
- GRP and epoxy are much more fragile and are best kept for the expert.

Daggerboard

A beginner's board should have a daggerboard, which should be fully retractable into the hull for sailing in shallow water or in strong winds.

Footstraps

Footstraps are not essential, but many boards come with them fitted: beginners are advised to remove them until they are ready for strong-wind sailing.

Mast track

Mast tracks are unnecessary for the beginner: if your board has one, leave it in a central position. Later, you can adjust it to balance the rig for different conditions and various wind directions.

The rig

Choice of a suitable rig is tremendously important. Sail size is the first consideration. If you intend to stick with one sail, go for a medium size: nothing is more dispiriting than pulling an oversize rig out of the water. For an adult choose something in the range 5.4 m^2 to 5.9 m^2, depending on your size and strength.

If you intend to windsurf often, you will need two sails: one of about 6 m^2 for light winds and the other, for stronger winds, of about 4.8 m^2, which is also fine for your first steps. The most economical way to buy them is to take a large sail with the board and add the small one later.

Boom

The modern tendency is for a short boom which makes the sail easier to manage and in particular aids pulling it out of the water. Try to get a boom no longer than 2.45 m, and consider paying extra for a variable length boom which will fit various sail sizes.

Try before you buy

You may find it helpful to try the equipment before buying so you can make sure the overall weight is not excessive for you, the sail is not too large and the board is sufficiently stable. If you plan to have lessons it might be wise to buy afterwards because the experience gained may influence your choice.

GETTING IT TOGETHER

1

2

3

4

1 Push the mast through the sleeve in the sail.
2 Insert the mast foot (and any extension tube) and loosely
tension the downhaul (use a loop in the rope as a purchase, if
necessary).
3 Stand beside the mast and note eye height. You should fix
the boom at this level.
4 Put the boom over the top of the mast.
5 Put the rig on the ground with the boom on top, lying along
the mast.

5

continued

6

7

8

9

10

11

12

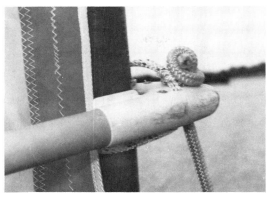

13

14

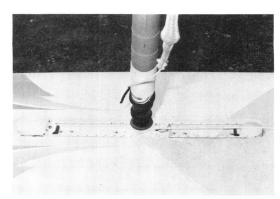

15

6,7   Make the inhaul rope into a loop and pass it down through one small hole in the boom end, round the mast, through the other small hole and over the knot.

8   Crank the boom carefully until it is at right angles to the mast. If the loop is too tight you will break the mast, but it should be tight enough for the boom to support itself horizontally in the correct position.

9   Attach the outhaul rope and half-tension it. Push the battens into place in the sail.

10,11   Tighten the outhaul until the vertical folds in the sail (behind the mast) disappear. Cleat the outhaul, and tie off.

12   Tension the downhaul until the horizontal creases in the sail disappear.

13   Knot the uphaul through its hole in the front of the boom. Clip the other end to the downhaul with a length of shock cord (elastic).

14,15   Push the mast foot into the board – normally in the front setting – and adjust until it fits firmly. Attach the safety leash. Check that the skeg is fitted into the bottom of the board. Push the daggerboard into its slot, and you are ready to go windsurfing.

2   Five-finger exercises

Position the board across the wind by aligning it at right angles to the flapping sail.

Before you take to the water, time spent practising handling the rig on shore – on the beach or even in your back garden – will pay immense dividends later. Whilst the sensation is not exactly the same as the real thing, the basics can be grasped at leisure and mistakes are not rewarded by an old-fashioned baptism!

If your first outing is on a course at a boardsailing school – a very worthwhile investment – then a dry-land simulator and a totally candid commentary will of course be provided.

Assuming a simulator is not available, remove the skeg and position the board *across* the wind.

Practising starting

Stand with your back to the wind. Place your feet, shoulder width apart, on the centreline of the board with one foot each side of the mast.

Hold the uphaul in both hands, pull up the sail and let it blow directly away from you like a flag. Stand up straight with your hips forwards, shoulders back and arms slightly bent.

Check which way the board is pointing: let's say to your right (as in the photographs). In this case your *right* hand is called your *front* hand, your *left* hand is your *back* hand. From now on we will only talk about front and back hands, because they then do the same job whichever way you're sailing.

Below: practising raising the rig and starting.

1 Transfer your front hand from the rope to the mast and let go with your back hand.

2 Move your back foot to the rear of the daggerboard case and your front foot just behind the mast, toes pointing forwards.

3 Turn your hips until you are facing the way you want to go.

4 With your front hand pull the rig across the board until it balances.

5 Put your back hand on the boom, level with your left shoulder.

6 Move your front hand from the mast to the front of the boom (the sail is still flapping).

7 Pull in with your back hand until the sail fills with wind. Your weight should be mainly on your back foot to counter the force of the sail. Stand up, push your hips forwards, arch your back and look in the direction you are 'sailing'.

The controls

Note how the wind varies in strength every few seconds. You will have to cope with these gusts and lulls.

If the pull of the sail increases, you can straighten your arms to open the gap between you and the mast and increase the weight you are applying to the sail. Similarly if the wind drops you can close the gap again to the original position (but not too close!)

Sailing is an ambidextrous sport; for every kilometre you sail you will have to sail a kilometre back in the opposite direction! So put in an equal amount of practice on either side of the sail.

In a gust, straighten your arms, and bend them in a lull.

3 A first sail

Above: take the rig to the water first, then go back for the board.

Below: getting on.

Now for the wet bit! Falling in is part of boardsailing: if you don't fall in occasionally you are not trying hard enough. But do make sure you are wearing a buoyancy aid and the right clothing and shoes (see page 46). Check the conditions are suitable (page 45), and sail with a companion.

Carrying

You won't be able to carry both board and rig together. If you launch the board first (and then go back for the rig), chances are you'll have to swim after it. So carry the rig into thigh-deep water with the mast foot towards the wind, and leave it while you go back for the board.

Fit the daggerboard and carry the board into the water on the upwind side of the rig. Fit the mast foot and safety leash and make sure the daggerboard is fully down.

Tethering

For your first attempt it is a good idea to attach a line to the board through the daggerboard case. The other end can be tied to a buoy or held by a friend on shore.

Mounting the board

Always climb onto the board from the side opposite the rig. Put your hands flat on the centreline, one each side of the mast foot.

Pull yourself out of the water until you are kneeling on the centreline. Grab the uphaul rope to give you a sense of security (false, sadly).

Stand up holding the uphaul, with the balls of your feet on the centreline. (You should be able to rock the board in either direction using your toes and heels.)

Exercises for balance

To gain confidence, drop the uphaul and try some of the following exercises.
1 See how close to the front and back of the board you can get.
2 Turn round to face the other way, then turn back again.
3 Jump (so both feet leave the board).

Note that the secret of staying dry is to keep your weight distributed evenly about the centreline. Relax your feet and legs, and don't try to correct every wobble of the board – or you will get cramp in your feet.

Raising the rig when it lies to leeward (that is, when your back is to the wind).

Raising the rig

This is one of the most strenuous parts of boardsailing, and good technique will avoid the risk of backache.

1 Check that the daggerboard is still fully down, and that the rig is lying away from the wind.

2 Stand with your feet shoulder-width apart, one each side of the mast foot.

3 Bend your knees to a right angle and grab the uphaul.

4 With your head up and your back straight, start to pull the rig up by straightening your legs.

5 Make sure that the mast stays at right angles to the board throughout – it should not lean towards the front or the back. Keeping the mast at right angles makes the board turn so it lies across the wind.

6 Continue to raise the mast by pulling in the uphaul rope hand-over-hand.

7 Transfer your front hand to the mast, just below the boom. Let go of the rope with your back hand. (Alternatively, transfer both hands to the mast, front hand above back hand.)

8 Stand up straight, shoulders back and arms extended. Look around, take a couple of deep breaths, and relax. This is the **secure position**, with the board at right angles to the wind.

Try this exercise for balance!

Raising the rig when it lies to windward (1), by allowing the wind to turn the board.

Raising the rig when it lies to windward (2), by allowing the rig to flip round.

Raising the rig when it lies to windward

Sometimes the rig ends up to windward of the board. When this happens you have two alternatives:

1 Pull the rig up a short way and at right angles to the board, and wait for the breeze to turn everything round so the top of the mast points away from the wind.

2 Pull the rig up quickly so that the wind catches it and flips it over the board, while you nimbly keep out of its way.

Once the mast is pointing away from the wind, you can raise the rig as before.

Turning the board

If you lean the rig towards the front of the board you will find the front swings round to meet it. If you lean the rig towards the back of the board the front will swing the other way. Practise turning the board by leaning the rig towards front and back and then return the board to a position at right angles to the wind — the secure position.

Turning the board round (to face in the opposite direction) is achieved by leaning the rig towards the back of the board. Keep the rig pointing in the same direction and shuffle your feet round the mast foot as the board turns.

To stop the turn, return the rig to the central position.

Now rotate the board 180 degrees in the opposite direction by once again raking the mast towards the back of the board.

Throughout these exercises remember to keep your arms slightly bent and to make small steps.

Below: turning the board by raking the rig forward, then back. Finally, holding the rig towards the back of the board turns the board through 180 degrees.

Starting off: choose a goal and sail towards it.

Bend your knees in a lull to bring your weight in over the board.

Now you are ready to go sailing!

Once you can get the board into the secure position you are ready to go sailing.

Choose a goal

Check that the board is at right angles to the wind, then sight along it to find a distant object in its path. This is your goal.

Move your rear foot to the back of the daggerboard case. Move your front foot behind the mast, toes forward.

Sail off

Check that the board is still pointing towards your goal (if necessary re-align it by raking the mast as on page 15).

1 Turn your hips until you are facing the way you want to go.

2 With your front hand pull the rig across the board until it balances.

3 Put your back hand on the boom, level with your shoulder.

4 Move your front hand from the mast to the front of the boom (the sail is still flapping).

5 Pull in with your back hand until the sail fills with wind. Your weight should be mainly on your back foot to counter the force of the sail.

6 Stand up, arch your back, flex your arms slightly and look at your goal.

7 If a gust pulls you forwards push away with your back hand to lessen the power in the sail before leaning further back and then pulling in again. If the gust is still too strong, let go with your back hand and let the sail flap. Then begin again at step 2.

8 In a lull stop yourself falling backwards by bending your knees as you pump with the sail (repeatedly pull in the boom with your back hand) to bring your weight over the centreline of the board. When you

are stable again ease your back hand out and resume your original position.

Try not to get locked-in to one position – the sail needs to be constantly adjusted.

9 Check you are still sailing towards your goal.

Problems with getting going

- Splashdown! If the sequence above doesn't seem to work, the first thing to check is the angle to the wind at which the board finishes up. The chances are it turned straight into the wind before unloading you, and the reason was that you had the sail raked too far back or you pulled in with both hands instead of just the back hand. The remedy is to push your front hand towards the front of the board as you pull in with your back hand.
- Not strong enough? The sail overpowers you every time you pull in. Starting a sailboard is like letting in the clutch on a car – do it too fast and you get a jerk. So pull in with the back hand gradually so the board can pick up speed a little at a time. Once you are moving the pull in the sail will seem much less.

  If you can't hold on, let go with your *back* hand – not the front one or the rig takes a nosedive, and you have to pull it out of the water all over again.
- *Position du cabinet*. Looks a strain and it sure is, particularly on the back. If you think you are overdoing the arching of your back you are probably in about the right position.
- Bend-ze-knees! Just like the skiing lesson. If you are being pulled forward don't lock at the knees and bend at the waist – you can't get back from that position. Instead arch your back and bend your knees with your hips forward – it is far more effective.

Position du cabinet!

Steering

So far we have assumed you are sailing straight towards your goal. Let's now suppose someone gets in your way and you have to avoid them. You can achieve this by turning towards the wind or away from it.

To turn towards the wind
1 Angle the mast towards the back of the board, swinging it across the front of your body.
2 Pull in a little with your back hand.
3 The front of the board will turn towards the wind. When you've turned enough to avoid the collision, push the rig forward to its original position and ease out your back hand a little.

You will now be travelling closer to the wind than before, and if you want to get back on course towards your goal you will need to turn away from the wind.

To turn away from the wind
1 Push the mast towards the front of the board.
2 Pull in with your back hand until the board turns.
3 When on course (towards the goal) return the rig to its original position, remembering to ease out the back hand.

Note:
● The mast position is important for turning, but it is pulling in with the back hand that makes the board turn.
● As the board turns away from the wind the power in the rig increases and you will need to lean back to compensate.
● The mast is moved fore-and-aft down the centreline of the board.
● When you turn towards the wind, don't overdo it. Remember: you can't sail straight towards the wind (see page 24).

Steering. In the sequence below the board turns first towards the wind, then away from it.

Sailing in a straight line

Tilting the rig back turns the board towards the wind

Tilting the rig forwards turns the board away from the wind

Above: turning round.

Getting back

Before you get too far from shore, you will want to stop and turn round.
1 Move your front hand onto the mast.
2 Let go with your back hand.
3 Take up the secure position with your feet either side of the mast.
4 You are now going to turn the board as you did on page 15. Lean the rig towards the back of the board.
5 Shuffle round the mast foot as the board turns. Note that *you* keep facing the same way (i.e. away from the wind) while the board turns to point back home.
6 Your new goal is the place you started from.

7 Now go through the usual starting procedure bearing in mind that you have a new front and back hand.

You should now be able to sail back to the point where you launched. But sometimes things go wrong, so it is wise to be familiar with the self-rescue techniques described on page 47 before going afloat.

Stopping

If you want to stop, let go with your back hand. The sail will swing away and flap, and the board will drift to a halt in the secure position.

If you need to stop more quickly let go of the rig altogether and jump backwards into the water grabbing hold of the board. You will stop immediately.

4 How it works

It is easy to understand how a board can sail directly away from the wind: it simply blows along like a feather on a pond – (a) in the first diagram. What is surprising is that the board can also sail across the wind (b), and even at an angle towards it (c). How is this possible?

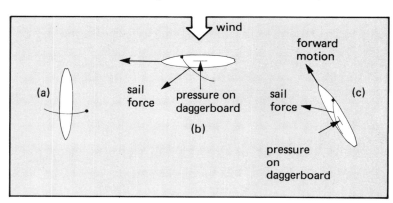

How does a board sail?

Unless the board is pointing away from the wind (a), the sail mainly pulls the board sideways. The daggerboard resists this: caught between these two forces the board takes the only way of escape and moves forwards, much as a piece of soap shoots out when squeezed between thumb and forefinger.

As the wind increases so does the force on the sail. To counteract this you must lean out, push with your legs and use your weight to counteract the power of the rig. The mast is now at an angle and the sail generates lift as well as forward power.

Steering

The force in the sail behaves as though it acts at one point, called the centre of effort (X in the diagram opposite). Similarly the sideways resistance of the board and daggerboard is focussed at the centre of lateral resistance (Y). The board pivots about Y.

- The board will sail in a straight line as long as X is directly above Y.
- If the rig is tilted forwards, X is in front of Y so the front of the board is pushed away from the wind.

sail
force

wind

weight

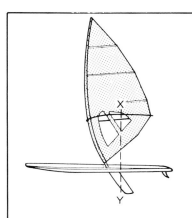

The board sails in a straight line when the wind pressure (acting at X) is directly above the water pressure (at Y)

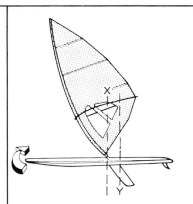

If the wind pressure is in *front* of the water pressure, the board turns *away* from the wind

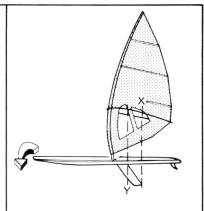

If the wind pressure is *behind* the water pressure, the board turns *towards* the wind

● When the rig is tilted backwards, X is behind Y and the back of the board is pushed away from the wind.

This principle applies for sailing in any direction, and is discussed further on page 32.

So far we have been sailing across the wind, known in the trade as *reaching*. Let's now look at boards sailing at other angles to the wind.

How close to the wind can I sail?

From a reach you can turn your board towards the wind (*luff up*) until you are sailing at about 45 degrees to it. That is as close as you can go, and you are now *sailing upwind* or *beating*. If you turned further you would enter the 'no-go zone' (below) – this is an arc of 90 degrees from the sailor, centred on the wind, within which the board will stop or even blow backwards. To sail upwind from A to B you need to sail a zig-zag course. Note that at the end of each 'zig' the board turns towards the wind – a beginner would do this as described on page 15 (turning the board) while a more experienced sailor would *sail* the board through the turn. This is known as a *tack*.

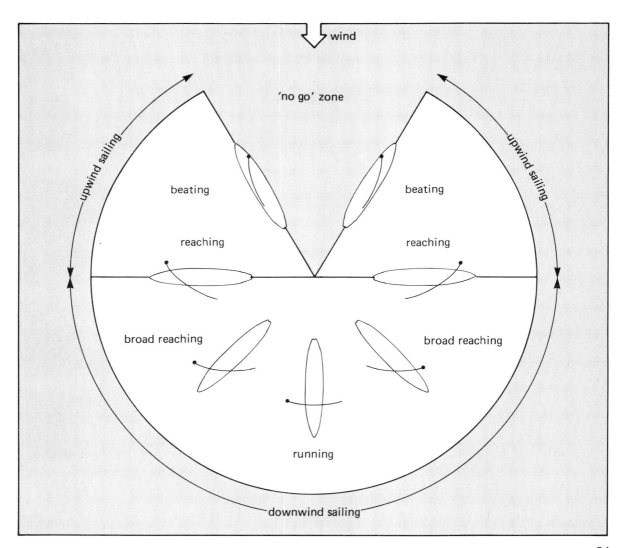

Sailing away from the wind

A board can sail at any angle away from the wind. Beginning as always from a reach, turn the board away from the wind (*bear away*) onto a broad reach — the fastest point of sailing. Bearing away further you eventually find yourself sailing away from the wind with the sail across the board: you are now *running*.

If you turn further you will need to swing the sail across the front of the board — this turn is a *gybe*.

To return to your starting point you will need to turn towards the wind and beat. This is shown in the last diagram, and the points of sailing are summed up opposite. Chapters 5 to 8 deal with each of these techniques in detail.

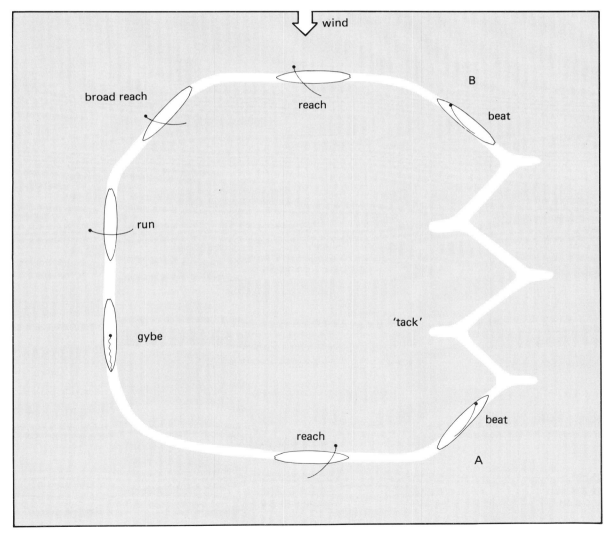

5   Upwind sailing

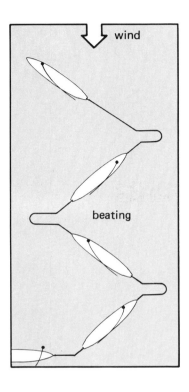

wind

beating

We have seen on page 24 that to gain ground towards the wind you need to beat. Here are some pointers to help you beat effectively.

1   Firstly, check that the daggerboard is fully down.

2   As with all boardsailing exercises, beginners should sail off on a reach. Now:

3   Lean the rig back and pull in with your back hand to turn the board towards the wind.

4   Continue to turn until the board is at 45 degrees to the wind. The boom will now be pulled in to the centreline. Keep the mast upright — don't let it lean away from you. You are beating.

5   Beginners often turn too far towards the wind and enter the no-go zone; this is shown up by the board slowing down (or stopping). To recover, tilt the rig forward to turn away from the wind, and allow the board to pick up speed again.

6   Your objective is to continue to sail close to the wind: not too close (or you stop), not too far off (or you make little progress to windward). Initially it may help you to stay on course if you sail towards an object on shore as a target. As you gain experience you can dispense with this, and keep trying to head closer to the wind (while still keeping speed up). In fact you will need to alter course often because the wind constantly changes its direction (and its speed for that matter).

7   After a while turn the board 'through' the wind and beat in the other direction.

8   After several zig-zags you should have made some progress towards the wind.

As you get better. . .

Experiment with different feet and hand positions.

- Try moving both feet out towards the rail, and up and down the board.
- Try holding the boom palm up (particularly with your front hand) to ease aching muscles.

Top row. Left: you can't sail close to the wind unless the boom is nearly on the centreline. Centre: this board is sailing too close to the wind – don't be too ambitious to start with. Right: this sail is stalled – the boardsailor has pushed too far with his front hand and pulled too much with his back hand.

Left: good upwind technique – feet out to the rail, and the front hand holding the boom palm up.

6 Tacking

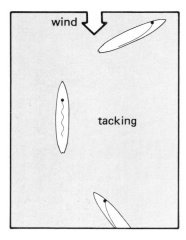

Until now, every time you turned the board around you stopped it. It's far more stylish (and efficient) to sail the board around – a manoeuvre known as tacking.

We show here a basic tack, followed by a speeded-up (jump) tack.

Basic tack

1   While sailing, put your front hand on the mast.
2   Hook your front foot around the mast. It is important that the ball of this foot finishes up on the centreline.
3   Look at the end of the boom and try to put this on the back of the board; this will make the board spin up into the wind. The pressure on your back hand mounts as the board turns: hang on!

Basic tack.

Jump tack.

4   The pressure gradually eases until the sail flaps (the board is now pointing into the wind). Now step smartly round the front of the mast, letting go with your back hand.
5   Change hands on the mast.
6   Lean the mast towards the front of the board (to continue the turn) as you shuffle round to the new secure position.
7   Now sail off as usual.

Jump tack

For an even faster turn try a jump tack. This is particularly useful when racing or out at sea, when the time you are unsupported by the sail must be reduced to a minimum.

The objective is to turn the board to its new course *before* you change sides.
1   Step back with your back foot and put all your weight on it as you lean the rig back and pull in hard with your back hand. The further back you can get your weight, the faster the board will turn.
2   As the board turns transfer your front hand to the mast and hook your front foot right round the front of the mast.
3   Continue to pull in the boom so the end swings across the back of the board and the front of the board turns right through the no-go zone.
4   Leap around the mast, to land with your feet in the new position.
5   Change hands on the mast and throw it well forward and to windward.
6   Transfer your back hand to the boom and pull in.
7   When the board is moving, transfer your front hand to the boom.
   Remember, don't shuffle round the mast! There should be no more than four steps. Count as you tack:
   One! Step back.
   Two! Foot around the mast.
   Three! Jump and land on new front foot.
   Four! New back foot lands.

7   *Offwind sailing*

Broad reaching
Broad reaching is the fastest and most exhilarating point of sailing. Since you are travelling at an angle away from the wind, make sure you can beat efficiently before setting off on a broad reach: you will have to beat for a long time to recover the ground lost to windward.

Bearing away
The technique for bearing away from a reach onto a broad reach or run is dealt with on page 32 (light winds) and page 39 (strong winds).

Position of the rig
The further off the wind you sail the squarer is the angle of the rig to the board, and the more the mast is raked to windward. The most extreme case would be the run, where the rig is straight across the board.

Balance
Downwind, the sail provides less of a counterweight to help you keep your balance, so you need to adopt a new stance. Move further back, angle the rig back towards you and put your feet near each rail as shown. Adjust the weight on each foot to trim the board flat.

Daggerboard
Less daggerboard is needed than when beating, indeed full daggerboard may at speed cause the windward rail to lift and unload the owner (a capsize fall). So use your toe to push the daggerboard handle forwards, partly retracting the blade. This also helps reduce any tendency of the board to turn towards the wind, because it moves the centre of lateral resistance back (page 23). Keep some daggerboard down, though, to aid stability; for light to moderate winds half-retracted is about right.

Opposite and below: good position on the reach.

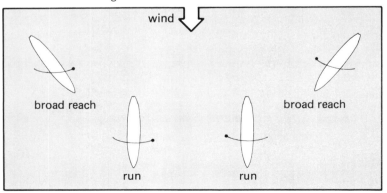

The main problem on the run is balance!

Below: turning onto a run.

Running

Running is the most difficult point of sailing because the sail cannot be used as an aid to balance; in waves this makes life very difficult.

Turning onto a run

1 From a reach rake the mast forward and pull in with your back hand.
2 As the board turns away from the wind, ease out your back hand to allow your front hand to angle the mast across the board.
3 Then pull in again with your back hand to drive the board round onto the run.
4 Finally, move both feet either side and to the rear of the daggerboard with your toes splayed out. Stand up straight, face forwards and look through the window in the sail. Angle the rig back towards you a little, with your arms and knees slightly flexed.

Steering on the run

The principle of steering is the same on the run as in other directions, but the practice is rather different. If you angle the rig to the left (keeping it square to the wind) the board will turn to the right, and vice versa. The reaction to steering is initially sluggish, and is helped by pushing down on the rails: push on the left foot to turn right, and vice versa.

Daggerboard

In light winds it is better to keep the daggerboard fully down for stability on the run.

As you get better. . . .

The main problem is balance. Once you have been thrown onto one leg it is hard to regain equilibrium without pushing harder on that leg – a sure recipe for falling in.

The key to this is to keep your weight central by flexing your knees and leaning into the roll early.

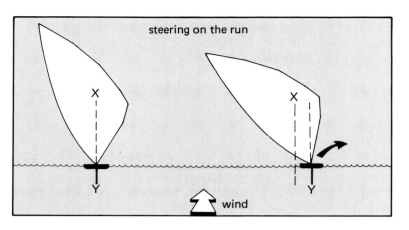

steering on the run

X

X

Y

Y

wind

Steering on the run.

Turning right.

Sailing straight.

Turning left.

8 Gybing

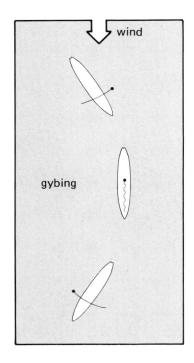

wind

gybing

So far, you have been turning the board by tacking – i.e. the front of the board turns into the wind (and the sail swings across the back).

Gybing is another way of turning in which the front of the board turns *away* from the wind (and the sail swings across the *front*). You will need this technique to change direction downwind.

Basic gybe

1   Turn the board away from the wind until you are sailing on a run.
2   Throw the boom away from you with your back hand (so it has the power to swing across the front of the board and out towards the new side). Transfer your back hand to the mast.
3   Let go with your front hand, and as the boom swings across to the new side grab the boom with it.
4   Pull in, and sail away.
5   When you are steady, transfer your front hand from the mast to the boom.

Hints

● If you have difficulty in restarting, go back to the secure position after step 2.
● The board will turn more easily if you push down on the outside foot (left foot in the photo sequence).
● At low speeds gybe with your daggerboard down, but at planing speeds retract it.
● You can make gybing easier by not only turning the board onto the run but continuing to turn it towards the new course before flipping the sail.

Below: gybing

9 Improving: strong-wind sailing

After you have mastered the basics you are ready to progress to the real thing – boardsailing in strong winds. Be careful: addiction is bound to follow!

When the wind is force 4 or above (over 20 km/hr) you can no longer stand vertically but will need to lean out with the rig supporting your weight. It's fantastic to fly the sail like this.

It is no good beginning in a hurricane – you will only become disheartened (not to mention waterlogged). Aim for a progression, building up your confidence in ever-increasing windspeeds.

And, of course, choose a safe location – your local lake is far more suitable than the open sea.

Despite this caution, a 'go for it' attitude is essential for strong-wind sailing. As with all good things in life you never get something for nothing – the trade-off for trying hard and falling in often is the joy of zooming over the water with the spray really flying.

Getting ready
Unpack your small sail (see page 6) and set it flat, i.e. pull all the control lines tight. Make sure you have read chapter 12; safety is important and with the wind high correct clothing is vital to combat the chill factor.

Make sure all your gear, particularly the mast foot and control lines, is in good order.

Below: starting in strong winds.
Opposite page: a beach start.

Starting off

In strong winds even pulling the sail up is difficult. With the rig partly out of the water pull it alternately towards the front and back of the board so the wind can get under the sail and help you raise it.

Once the sail is up, avoid letting the boom end touch the water (which would allow the wind to blow the sail flat again).

The next stage is perhaps the hardest for the beginner. To get moving:

1 Take your back foot well back.
2 Brace your front foot against the mast foot.
3 *Rake the rig well over towards the wind.*
4 Bend your back knee – get really low.
5 Straighten your front leg and push with it.
6 Pull in with your back hand.

Hints

- It is the difference in speed between the board and the wind that causes the problems. Once the board is moving fast life becomes easier. . . and more exciting.
- If you find that pulling in the sail simply jerks you forwards, try building up speed more gradually by repeatedly pulling in and relaxing your back hand.
- Falling in backwards is a good sign – you are trying hard. But if you fall forwards, commit your weight more to the rig.
- You may find the board turns into the wind and unloads you backwards into the oggin. Chances are you are leaning towards the back of the board instead of committing yourself to lean out over the side. Get lower, and rake that rig towards the wind.
- In really strong winds retract the daggerboard a little, and make sure the mast foot is in the front position.

Beach start

The beach start is a good method of setting off from the shore, particularly when there are waves.

1 Position the board across the wind with the mast lying along it and the boom pointing away from the wind.
2 Stand between the rig and the wind and pick up the rig with your front hand, holding the mast just above the boom.
3 Pick up the board with your back hand so the board is on edge with the deck towards you.
4 Push the board into knee-deep water and transfer both hands onto the boom.
5 The daggerboard stays retracted throughout the start.
6 The board will try to turn into the wind at this stage, so put pressure on the mast foot by pushing on the boom and making a circular movement with it; first away from you and then downwind. The board will pivot about its skeg and move into deeper water.
7 Once the board is in a broad reach position it will be some distance from you. Pull it directly back towards your body.
8 Put your back foot onto the centreline just in front of the rear footstrap (if any).

37

9 With the board still pointing away from the wind step up *and forward*.

10 Once your front foot is on the board you can pull in the sail (to keep your balance) and sail off. Note that the sail is not used to pull you onto the board – if you try this the board will take off without you and you will simply fall backwards.

Stance on different points of sailing

Keep your arms straight because they will soon get tired if bent. A harness (page 42) will increase your sailing endurance considerably.

Upwind

Move your feet to the windward edge of the board to hold down the rail. If the board still tries to rail up, retract the daggerboard a little. Try to keep the board planing fast rather than sailing it close to the wind and losing speed.

Reaching

Like a thoroughbred racehorse, a sailboard is very sensitive to the controls at speed. A good sailor appears to race along making no apparent adjustments to the rig. This is deceptive – in fact you need to make continual small alterations so the mast stays at a constant distance from your body.

When the wind increases ease out your back hand to spill the wind for a fraction of a second – this allows the rig plus your body to fall back to the required position. Pulling in again with your back hand powers up the sail once more to hold you in the new stance.

Bearing away.

If the wind drops pull in with your back hand to come more upright, if necessary bending your knees sharply to move your weight towards the centre of the board.

On standard boards put one foot on each side – the front foot on the windward rail pointing forward and the back foot on the leeward rail at 90 degrees to the centreline. Use your feet to keep the board flat. On funboards this is the moment to use the rear set of straps.

Adjust the daggerboard so it is possible to sail towards your objective without the board lifting onto one rail – in very strong winds this will usually mean fully retracting the blade. With a following sea retract the daggerboard if the board keeps turning into the wind.

Running

In strong winds, particularly on the sea, running is difficult because you can't use the rig for balance.

Keep your toes turned out (if possible curl them round the rail) and pull the rig back towards you. Position yourself according to wind-strength: too far forward and you will be unable to hold on when a gust arrives or will be dragged forward, too far back and the tail sinks, making the board oversensitive to rail steering and increasing the pull of the rig. If the wind is really strong kneel on one knee (or in extreme cases lie down) to reduce the projected sail area (see diagram). Bend your arms to a right angle so you can absorb the power of the gusts.

The main problem is that when the board rolls your weight is thrown onto the lower edge, which turns the board and makes the roll worse. Avoid this by leaning your weight into the roll *early*: successful running is a question of anticipation.

Keep the daggerboard down for stability on the run, unless the board is planing fast or following waves are making it pivot about the daggerboard and turn up into the wind.

So much for the various points of sailing. The next problem is how to turn from one to another.

Good stance for upwind sailing (top) and running (above).

Bearing away

Making the board turn away from the wind is one of the most difficult manoeuvres for the aspiring strong-wind sailor. There are two ways of doing this; firstly, let's look at how to turn the board using the rig. In the next section (flare gybing) we'll see how to use the rails as well.

Turning to a broad reach

1 Retract the daggerboard.
2 Rake the rig to windward (not forward).
3 Bend your back knee to lower your weight – in a real screamer you will almost be sitting on the board.
4 Pull in with your back hand. The board will now squirt round away from the wind. If you simply hold this position you will be catapulted forwards. So . . .
5 Ease out your back hand, then repeat steps 2 to 5 until you have reached the required course.

Bearing away like this in a series of 'bites' reduces the chance of a catapult fall (in which the rig flings you over the front of the board before you have a chance to let go).

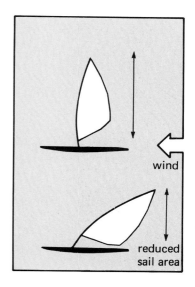

wind

reduced sail area

Above and opposite: the flare gybe.

Practising foot steering.

Turning from a broad reach to a run

If you want to turn further, to a run, the final stage is tricky because the apparent wind in the sail dies almost to nothing (since you are travelling in the same direction as the true wind). If you are caught leaning out at this stage a watery reception awaits you.

1 Try to anticipate the problem and let the rig pull your weight onto the centreline before the apparent wind drops away.

2 Move into the strong-wind running position (see above) before the rig regains power (and jerks you forward).

Flare gybe

In this gybe the board is turned by using the rails, while the rig controls the power until the gybe is complete.

The daggerboard can be up (strong winds) or down (moderate winds).

1 From a reach, rake the mast towards the wind.

2 Step back with your front foot so both feet are in the running position.

3 Push down on the windward rail and pull in with your back hand, tilting the mast forwards and towards the wind.

4 Lean your body into the turn.

5 Continue to rake the mast further across the board while pulling in with your back hand (to keep the sail full of wind).

6 When the board has turned sufficiently, flatten it by stepping forward onto your new front foot.

7 You are now sailing clew-first (i.e. with the battens pointing into the wind). Let the board pick up a little speed.

8 Release the back hand to let the sail flip round. Take this hand to the mast.

9 Let go with your front hand. Pull the mast to windward.

10 Sail off in the normal way.

To practise flare gybing turn onto a run and stand half a metre further back than normal. Practise turning the board to left and right using the rails, keeping the rig square to the wind. As you get better turn the

40

board through a wider angle and stand further back to sink the tail and increase sensitivity. From full speed an expert can leap to the back of the board (which will stop it almost dead), then spin the board on its tail and sail off in the opposite direction!

Gusts

Gusts are both the agony and the ecstasy of windsurfing. Depending on your skill you can either accelerate off in a shower of spray, or fall off (also in a shower of spray).

A gust is a band of stronger wind which shows itself as a tell-tale dark streak moving over the water's surface. In a gust the wind direction may change quite substantially; keep looking to windward for an approaching gust so you will be prepared when it hits you.

If you are sailing upwind, turn downwind a few degrees as each gust approaches. This enables the board to pick up speed and allows for the

Harness technique: jerk the boom so the line swings onto the hook or off it.

Arrange the harness line symmetrically about the balance point.

wind coming further ahead (which would backwind the sail if you stay on the old course). Crouch low and get ready to take the strain! When the board is up to its new speed turn back to a windward course.

Offwind simply lower your weight so you can combat the gust more easily when it strikes. Your aim is to enjoy the blast, using it to make the board go much faster.

On the run, eyes in the back of your head are useful! Pump the boom towards you just before the gust strikes to increase speed and to rake the rig towards the back of the board.

Harness technique

A harness increases many times your endurance in strong winds. It takes the strain off your arms by allowing you to hang your body weight from the boom. Several different types are available; the one shown here consists of a hook which fits over lengths of rope tied underneath the boom.

The position and length of the ropes are matters of personal preference. As a guide find the balance point of the rig (the point where you can hold the boom with one hand when the sail is full of wind). Next, hold the boom comfortably with your hands equally spaced about the balance point. Finally attach the rope just inside your hand positions. Repeat on the other side.

Adjust the length of each line so that your elbows are bent at right angles when you are hooked on.

Practise using the harness in moderate winds onshore before you go afloat. With the rig full of wind, jerk the boom towards you so that the line swings into the harness hook, and then lean back. Now you are connected to the boom you will have to cope with gusts and lulls by using your legs to position your body.

42

The only way to get off the hook is to pull yourself towards the boom. This is made somewhat harder when you are catapulted forwards through the air: if you are getting into trouble, or plan to tack or gybe, unhook early.

Use the harness at first when beating; with practice you will also be able to use it when reaching.

Footstraps and mast tracks

The two most common questions our funboard pupils ask are 'Why are my footstraps set too far back?' and 'When should I use the mast track?' In fact neither straps nor track are much use to you until the wind reaches force 4 (20 km/hr).

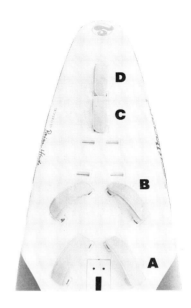

- For upwind sailing on all-round funboards your back foot is normally in strap B (see illustration) and your front foot is free. The mast track is in the front position.
- On a beam reach with the daggerboard retracted your back foot will be in C, your front foot in A and the track in the middle position.
- On a broad reach you can get into straps D and B, with the mast at the back.
- On a run you don't use the straps.

Once in the straps you must adopt a new stance to prevent the tail sinking: hang your weight forward from the boom, using the mast foot as a third foot. Once the board is planing properly you will be able to steer by banking the board into the turns like a waterskier. Note that the daggerboard must be fully retracted.

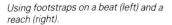

Using footstraps on a beat (left) and a reach (right).

Landing: this is the technique to use in waves.

Landing

At the end of your heavy-weather session you will no doubt want to come ashore without being munched by the breaking waves.

1 Sail into shallow water with your daggerboard retracted.

2 Jump off before you lose your skeg in the sand.

3 Hold the rig by the mast using your front hand.

4 Pick up the back of the board with your back hand (as for launching) and push it clear of the surf.

10 Where and when to sail

The boards are on the roof for your first session at the coast. You've remembered to bring the beer and the suntan oil. But what else do you need to think of before setting off?

Weather

TV, radio, telephone forecast services and weather forecasts in newspapers are all good sources of information. Find out the wind's expected speed and direction in your sailing area, and see if any nasties are forecast such as fronts, gales or thunderstorms.

Wind strength
For the inexperienced, 8 to 15 km/hr of wind is quite sufficient (Force 2 to 3).

Wind direction
When you arrive at the coast your choice of alternatives might look like those on the map shown. With car parks at A, B, C, and D, where are you going to park and launch?

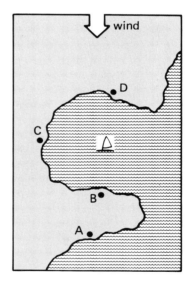

A is definitely out. The wind is blowing directly offshore and if anything at all goes wrong – you break some gear or get tired – your next port of call may be on the other side of the ocean.

B is safe but tricky. After you have pulled the board into waist-deep water, got on and pulled up the sail, you will hear a nasty scraping noise as the daggerboard grounds back on the shore.

D is safe (if anything goes wrong you will wash up on the shore at B) but not ideal. It may be sheltered by trees or houses and the wind gusty. The true wind force will not be apparent until you have got out into the bay, by which time you may find it too strong for you, particularly as you will have to sail back upwind. You will almost inevitably end up landing at C and walking home!

C is the best. With a sideshore wind you can reach out and back from the beach in the easiest direction, and if anything goes wrong you will end up on the shore at B.

Tides

Tides can be a very important factor in deciding where to sail. You can find out about them by buying a set of tide tables for a few pence – this is well worth while. Of the two tides a day the dangerous part to the boardsailor is the ebb or outgoing tide, which is particularly strong in the middle two hours of its six-hour period. Geographically it is strongest in places where the tidal flow is compressed – such as in

Self rescue.

estuaries, deep-water channels, mouths of harbours and off headlands.

You can tell tidal direction by looking at moored boats, which usually swing down-tide of their anchor, or buoys which lean down-tide, and may have a bow-wave on the other side. Also you can tell if the tide is on its way out by the wet sand left behind.

A combination of wind and tide can push novice windsurfers away from their launch site amazingly fast.

Common sense

Windsurfing is a safe sport if a few rules and a little common sense are applied.

1   Don't sail alone. There are circumstances where you can be separated from your board and if you are alone this can be fatal. A friend can always give you a lift or raise the alarm.

2   Tell someone you are going (and check in when you get back).

3   Wear the right clothes. Always wear a buoyancy aid. In summer you will need a long-john wetsuit at least, plus a windproof top and a pair of soft-soled shoes.

In winter sport a steamer or drysuit with thermal underwear. Warm boots, hat and gloves are also essential.

4   Check your equipment before you go out, particularly the lines and the mast foot. The rig must have a safety leash to prevent the board and rig separating. (In surf this should be a long line attached to the nose of the board which will then float down-surf of the rig, without the two becoming entangled.)

In the pack on the back of your harness carry spares lines, a spare mast foot, some money and some red flares (preferably smoke flares). In heavy conditions include a 4-metre tow line in case of rescue (see opposite page).

5   Don't sail too far from shore. Don't go further than you can paddle home.

6   Areas to avoid: swimming beaches (if there are windsurfing lanes, stick to them), commercial traffic lanes (watch out for ferries in particular) and boats racing. Although you have certain rights, in general Might is Right.

Tide rips (e.g. at the mouth of a harbour) are bad news. Give divers' boats a wide berth – they will be flying a blue and white swallowtail flag.

7   Watch for changes in the weather: a huge black cloud approaching usually means trouble.

8   Look for a landmark when setting out from shore and keep an eye on it – it is easy to become disorientated on the water.

9   Use a sensibly sized sail. If you are caught out with too large a sail up, reef it either by pushing the foot of the sail up the mast to the boom or by crimping the sail to the mast at two-thirds height, lashing it in place with one of your spares lines.

10   Tiredness. If you start falling in too often, come ashore before exhaustion sets in.

11   Hypothermia. Drowsiness, fatigue, lack of interest, slow reactions, confusion and slurred speech are signs that the blood flow to the outer limbs is becoming restricted and the body's core is beginning to cool. If you suspect this is happening head for shelter. Wrap yourself in blankets, have a hot non-alcoholic drink and summon medical assistance. Watch out for other sailors suffering from these symptoms.

In trouble on the water?

Always stay with the board — never leave it to swim ashore, for example. It will support you, and you can paddle it faster and further than you can swim.

If the board and rig becomes separated stick with the board (which would otherwise blow away) and paddle it after the rig.

Self rescue

If the wind is onshore, simply blow ashore by standing holding the uphaul, letting the sail flap in front of you like a flag.

If the wind is blowing roughly parallel to the shore, point the board towards the shore and pull the sail nearly up, letting the back corner trail in the water. The sail will partly fill, making you scud over the water surprisingly fast.

If the wind is offshore, furl the sail as follows:
1 Detach the mast foot and safety leash.
2 Undo the outhaul.
3 Remove full-length battens and stow them down the back of your wetsuit.
4 Roll the sail tightly and tie it using the uphaul and outhaul ropes.
5 Kneel on the board with the rig across it at right angles.
6 Swing the rig around so the mast lies down the centreline, mast foot forward. Kneel (or in rough conditions lie flat) and paddle with your hands and forearms.

Being rescued

1 Summon help by waving your outstretched arms up and down (the international distress signal). If you can't be seen, wave something. Alternatively let off a flare.
2 Once you have been seen by rescuers, roll up the sail as described above.

Rescue by another board
There are two methods:
1 Towing alongside. Here you hold on to the rescuer's mast foot. This works well for light conditions and short distances.
2 In heavy conditions it is better to be towed astern. A 4-metre tow line should be carried, which can be attached to the mast foot of the towing board, passed through the towing eye on your board and the end held in your hand. (If you fall off, simply let go the rope and your board is left to support you.)

With both these methods it is possible to tack, so upwind progress can be made.

Above: the international distress signal. Below: being rescued.

11   Rules of the road

The rules of sailing are the same for sailboards as for any other sailing boat. A full discussion of them is outside the scope of this book, but there are three key rules you should know to keep you from doing much damage to your fellow sailors.

Boards meeting on opposite tacks

A board is either on port tack or starboard tack. You are on port tack if your left hand is your 'front' hand; you are on starboard if your right hand is your 'front' hand. *A port tack board must keep clear of a starboard tack board.* Boards D, E and F are on port tack in the diagram and must keep clear of boards A, B and C which are on starboard.

Boards meeting on the same tack

If the boards are overlapped – i.e. if the bow of the following board is ahead of a line at right angles to the back of the leading board – then the *windward board must keep clear of the leeward board.* Board G must keep clear of H, I must keep clear of J and K must keep clear of L.

If the boards are *not* overlapped, then the *board clear astern must keep clear of the board clear ahead.* N is overtaking and must not sail into the back of M.

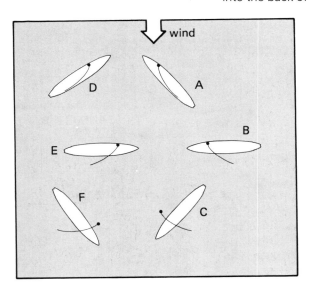

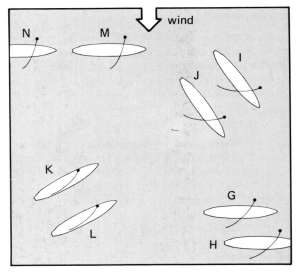